66 WAYS TO BECOME A MILLIONAIRE

MOON MERCHANT

Contents

Contents

Contents

1

Affiliate Marketing

If you already have a website that's driving in targeted traffic, a great way to make passive income from the content you're already creating as an easy side business idea is through affiliate marketing. ShareASale, Rakuten, Clickbank, and Skimlinks are a few of the best affiliate networks and tools that can help you make money from the content you already produce, thus amplifying your side business idea income. Check out this extensive list by Justine Grey, covering the 59 Best Affiliate Programs for Business Bloggers to get some inspiration on how other bloggers are growing affiliate blogs from side business ideas to full-time companies.

2

Amazon Reselling

Anyone can sell goods on Amazon, provided you have products to sell (or buy low, then resell). If you're the type to hit all the local garage sales each weekend, there are all sorts of valuable things that can be resold online as a side business idea. If you want to step your Amazon selling game up, check out this detailed guide to Amazon and eBay retail arbitrage on Entrepreneur featuring an interview with Julie Becker and several drop-shippers who've grown this home based business idea from a side business idea into a lucrative money-maker.

3

Develop an App

Sometimes it seems like there's an app for everything. Yet somehow, new ones keep popping up and selling for lots of money, all the time. If you spot a niche that hasn't been filled to its potential just yet, and you can learn the coding skills (or know someone who already has them), you could be on to something with this side business idea. Today, it's even possible to build an app without any coding skills whatsoever. Just make sure you validate your app idea before jumping too far in. Even if your app business idea doesn't pan out to be a best seller, you'll still pick up valuable skills.

Listen to my interview with serial entrepreneur and investor, Michele Romanow about how she built an app that earned $500,000 in 3 months (as a side business idea outside of her day job) and how she eventually sold the company to Groupon. It's seriously incredible.

4

Start a YouTube Channel

Yes, spending time on YouTube can be a legitimate business idea if you take it seriously. If you can create value-driven, entertaining video content and grow your subscriber base to a few thousand subscribers, your videos can start generating pretty substantial income from all the ads being displayed on your videos. Many YouTube users make well into the millions each year, so there's clear potential to take this from side business idea to eventual millionaire with the right combination of content, audience, skills, relationships, and timing. If you're considering starting a YouTube channel it's important to use best practices when making videos. Read the YouTube playbook for tips that will result in the faster growth of your channel. Additionally, think about investing in a quality camera and microphone since the production quality of videos can often affect your viewership.

5

Wedding Planning

Like birthdays, marriages happen all the time. This means you can treat weddings as a recurring fountain of business opportunities: wedding dresses and coats, jewelers, food caterers, venue providers, photographers and videographers, performers, flower shops, travel agencies, souvenir crafts, and a host of other ventures. Now imagine if you can form a network of these service providers so you can offer engaged couples a range of hassle-free wedding packages as a turnkey business idea. The process is certainly fun (and time-consuming), but as a side business idea, the pay can be pretty great.

6

T-Shirt Printing Business

As I've already covered with TeeSpring, the T-shirt retailing business is worth millions of dollars. But what if you want to do the manufacturing side of things? T-shirt printing turns out to be quite a rewarding business idea for many each year, but can quickly consume much of your side business idea time—so know what you're getting into before diving in. This multi-billion dollar industry counts big corporate factories as well as home-based part-time entrepreneurs.

7

Home-Based Makeup Services

If you have a talent for helping people look their best, and know how to mesmerize with eyeliners and turn heads with lipsticks, consider using your beauty skills to pursue this easily profitable side business idea. For under $2000, you can start your own make-up artist business which can make for the foundation of a potentially lucrative side business idea that turns a profit largely by referrals and word-of-mouth from your happy customers.

8

Buying and Selling Cars

Car flipping can be a fun way to turn your love for cars into a quick side business idea if you have the capital and a stomach for the inherent risk. Buying and selling cars is similar to other "buy low, sell high" business models, but the profit potential per hour invested can be very high. According to Jeremy Fisher at 3HourFlip.com, the trick is to learn how to make car deals come to you, so you can minimize your time invested and maximize your profit on each flip with this side business idea.

9

Recycling

Though certainly not for everyone, recycling the containers from products left strewn around on the ground can become a surprisingly decent side business idea if you put in the time. Attending events like street fairs and outdoor concerts can be a great starting place. Put on a clean shirt, jeans, apply your sunscreen, grab a cheap pick-up tool like this one, sturdy plastic bags, and you can sell them for upwards of $4.00/pound on eBay.

10

Selling Life Insurance

Are you an extrovert that loves meeting new people? Selling insurance products—particularly life insurance—may be a great way to bring in some extra cash and build residual income in your spare time. Selling life insurance on the side could quickly generate a consistent $1,000 - $2,000 per month depending on how much time you invest in this side business idea. To get started you'll likely want to take an online course to brush up on the subject matter, and then pass a state licensing exam. The biggest challenge you'll face as a new agent is generating sales beyond just helping out friends and family. From there, it's all about networking and lead generation to grow this one. Learn more about this side business idea with this getting started in life insurance guide from the team over at NoExam.

11

Online Courses

Using your skills for profit is a common trend with all of the best side business ideas. If you're an expert at something, there's likely an audience of people online who would be willing to pay to become an expert in your field—just like you. If you want to take your skills and turn them into an online course that teaches others how to get the same results you've achieved in your life, career, or business, start with How to Create an Awesome Online Course on Udemy, where the instructor Miguel Hernandez covers how he makes over $90,000/yr teaching online. You'll learn from more than 8 hours of video instruction.

If you want to find a profitable online course idea in the next 3 days, join my free online course Find a Profitable Business Idea today. It'll walk you step-by-step through the process I've used to generate more than $15,000 in online course sales in a single week. Then once you're ready to start teaching your own online course, I recommend using Teachable, the easiest and most affordable platform to use for creating, hosting and selling your online courses. They also have a ton of free educational resources about how to get started with creating an online course (yes, even as a side business idea) when you sign up.

12

Graphic Design

While having a formal background in graphic design is absolutely going to be helpful, it's also relatively easy to learn the foundations of graphic design on your own. An increasingly easy-to-use Adobe Illustrator and even more easily accessible tools like Stencil and Visme are making it so that just about anyone with two opposable thumbs, a bit of creativity, and motivation can earn a side income doing things like designing (and selling) images like these motivational quotes that can be printed onto posters and sold on platforms like Etsy. Or you can find a local startup, small business owner, or photographer who could benefit from some extra help designing or altering images. But before you can graduate from side business idea and start earning a full-time living as a graphic designer, you'll need to build your skills—I recommend starting with reading the foundational book Graphic Design School and Steal Like an Artist, the incredible book by Austin Kleon about how to become more creative. To accelerate your education in becoming a graphic designer even quicker, check out the online courses Graphic Design Fundamentals and The Graphic Design Bootcamp. Then once you're an expert at your craft, you can further your education and move up to offering more hands-on experiences like design sprints for higher-value clients around the world.

13

Start a Blog

Think blogging is no longer a viable source of income? Think again. Tens of thousands of bloggers (including yours truly) are creating profitable content on topics as diverse as scrapbooking, home cooking, travel, film, lifestyle, business, personal finance, and more. And we're growing our blogs into six-figure businesses thanks to a combination of email subscribers, affiliate marketing, blog sponsorships, and other revenue streams. Your first step with starting a blog is quickly getting the technical side of things handled (my free master course on blogging will show you how), and then both understanding what your audience craves and learning how to attract those readers online.

If you want to speed up the process of launching your blog, I recommend setting up quick, affordable, and easy website hosting with a company like Bluehost, choosing a simple WordPress theme, and working on your first post, in order to set the precedent of prioritizing your time on creating content, connecting with (and building) your audience. Then once you've been able to build a community around your blog, you'll want to invest in really understanding your readers—so that you can give them more of what they want.

14

Web Design

Web designers are incredibly valuable for technology companies—which is why becoming a freelance web designer is a top side business idea today. Web design is all about mastering the art of creating a beautiful, value-driven experience for the people using a website or app. There are always new websites popping up in need of professional web design, and foundational books like HTML & CSS: Design and Build Websites by acclaimed web designer Jon Duckett and Don't Make Me Think by user experience legend Steve Krug will get you started down the right path to quickly determining whether or not becoming a web designer is a viable side business idea for you.

Then you can move into more actionable online courses like Modern Web Design on CreativeLive and Learn Web Design and Profitable Freelancing on Udemy will teach you everything from foundational web design knowledge to earning your first freelance income as a web designer. On top of that, you can take even more immersive courses and learning experiences with access to direct instructor feedback and personal mentorship with platforms like Treehouse, LinkedIn Learning and General Assembly to get up-to-speed even quicker with this career path and listen to my podcast interview with Ian Paget about how to become

***a freelance designer* as a side business idea.**

15

Web Development

As a web developer, you'll build incredibly valuable skills that are in extremely high demand. You can get up to speed on building websites in as little as a few months with inexpensive or free online education programs like Treehouse, the Web Developer Bootcamp on Udemyand Codecademy.

If you don't find what you're looking for there, here's a list of the 45 best places you can learn to code for free. Once you command a knowledge of HTML, Ruby, Python, Javascript, or CSS, you can start a freelance business as a side business idea to build your portfolio while you still hold onto your full-time job. Listen to my podcast interview with Laurence Bradford about her journey to become a freelance web developer, too. And over time, you'll build more relationships, have more experience and eventually take this side business idea over to becoming a full-time source of income.

Packaging your skills and knowledge into a downloadable eBook that delivers value to those seeking to learn a skill, advance in their careers, or start their own businesses, makes for a strong value proposition if you target the right audience. Check out Leslie Samuel's great guide to selling eBooks online and start building your strategy around this side business idea. This class with Tara Gentile on CreativeLive will also show you how to use your existing body of work to write an eBook within the next week. Put in some serious work with your eBook, build an audience and you'll have a platform to pitch traditional publishers on landing a book deal—then you can write one of the best business books and really build your personal brand.

17

Instagram Marketing

Build up a following on your Instagram account and you could quickly be approached by major brands, gear companies, and other relevant businesses that sell products or services related to the type of content you share on Instagram—creating multiple potential side business ideas that'll come to you. If you have the right marketing skills and hundreds of thousands of followers, you can easily charge anywhere between $500 to $5,000 per post (or more)—which makes for a very profitable side business idea. Check out this fashion Instagrammer on ThePennyHoarder, making a significant income from brand sponsorships. Once you get some traction, to cut down on the amount of time you spend uploading images, you can make your entire workflow more efficient by posting photos from your Mac or PC

18

Online Coaching

If you have something you're skilled at and very passionate about, you can turn that winning combination into offering your services with one-on-one online coaching as a solid side business idea. Just be sure to implement your own opportunity management system so you don't get caught up working with clients that you can't measurably help. Elmira Strange will give you a step-by-step plan for putting your skills and experience to work by developing an online coaching business—even as a side business idea in the time around your full-time job—so be sure to check out her course on Udemy for a jump start on this side business idea.

On top of just the skill and experience components to being a successful online coach, this side business idea is all about building a community around the help you're offering and fostering trust with members. Plus, your community members will learn from each other along the way. Creating the space for that community can be as simple as setting up a private Facebook group or choosing a community-building platform like Ning.com that has even more capabilities like using your own custom URL, having internal forums, customized designs, and more.

19

Podcasting

If you can create a regular audience for your podcast on a specific topic, this is a great way to get sponsors and fund this side business idea. My podcast, The Side Hustle Project is actually my current side business idea, and because I had an existing audience here on my blog at the time I launched the show, I was able to broker a $5,000 sponsorship from Freshbooks to place ads on the first ten episodes before I even got started.

When I used to work at CreativeLive, I regularly paid $250-$500 (or even much more depending upon audience size) per episode for 90 seconds worth of advertisements on relevant podcasts like The Tim Ferriss Show, the #1 business podcast right now from the 4-Hour Workweek author, Tim Ferriss. The podcast has even helped Tim launch his latest New York Times bestseller, Tools of Titans to a wider readership.

Naturally, it helps if you already have an online audience you can tap for listening to your regular podcast (like I did), but that hasn't stopped thousands of people from building successful side business ideas into lucrative podcasts—including Alex Blumberg, founder of Gimlet

***Media** who teaches **how to use storytelling and launch a podcast**. You can also check out this class from podcaster and entrepreneur, Lewis Howes, about **how to make money podcasting** as a side business idea, which regularly broadcasts for free on CreativeLive.*

20

Local Business Consulting

If you've developed valuable skill sets or certifications within your industry over the years, consider putting your skills to use in your free time by offering your consulting services to local business owners as a potentially lucrative side business idea. Whether you're an expert marketer, business strategist, or manufacturing aficionado, there's likely a local business owner who's willing to pay you to help them solve an issue with their company—if you can craft an effective cold email that convinces them to hire you. Start with this 18-step checklist to becoming a local business consultant as a side business idea, from Karyn Greenstreet. When you're ready to get serious about becoming a consultant, check out all of my picks for the best online business courses to keep building your skills and learning how to land your first consulting clients. Personally, I think this is one of the best business ideas you can get started with today.

21

Phone Case Business

There's a huge growing market for mobile phone accessories, and plenty of handmade sellers are raking in 6 and sometimes 7 figures from their phone case businesses. You can get your own phone case business up and running as a side business idea in a matter of days with turnkey solutions from Case Escape, my previous company, and you can now get ready-to-go kits that'll give you everything you need to start a phone case business. Once you're up and running, you can sell cases on Etsy, Amazon Handmade, and Fancy. During our first year of selling phone cases as a side business idea on our Etsy store, we made around $60,000 in revenue from that selling channel alone—not to mention additional sales from fairs, trade shows, promotional products vendors, parties, events and other online marketplaces. From there, the sales only continued growing and we graduated from side business idea to full-time company that I ran with my best friend for multiple years.

22

Commission-Only Sales

If you have a knack for connecting with people and the willingness to take on some risk, a commission-based freelance sales role could be a great side business idea for you. Many startups seek part-time and commission-only salespeople, especially when they're just getting started, which means you'll often be able to make this a home-based business idea. Develop your sales strategies, become an inside sales rep and perfect your cold calling skills on the side in your free time for nothing but commission, negotiate a little equity and you could profit big time if you're pitching a solid product and the startup succeeds. Start your sales education with the acclaimed books, Secrets of a Master Closer and To Sell is Human by famed bestselling author Daniel Pink and you'll be well on your way to getting this side business idea off the ground.

Then you can move on to more immersive sales education through online courses like Sales Training and Prospecting on Udemy, The Guide to Pitching, and Selling Clients on CreativeLive. Once you're ready to put your selling skills to the test, check out Angel List and see if any sales position opportunities align with your interests—the last thing you want to do is get stuck selling products or services you're not interested in. However, starting out your sales career

as a side business idea gives you the flexibility to easily change courses if you ever need to.

23

Virtual Assistant

Have a knack for staying organized? If you're a jack of all trades, you should consider working as a virtual assistant as a side business idea. You can find great gigs on Elance, Indeed, or Upwork. It can be an awesome way to rub shoulders with some very important people, build up your professional network, develop in-demand new skills (like creating GIFs and VR videos), grow your side business idea and you'll have the added perk of being able to start this as a home based business idea. Becoming a virtual assistant can be a particularly great side business idea if you're hoping to travel the world while making money online as a digital nomad.

24

Tax Preparation

It's not the sort of side business idea that's covered in glory, but someone needs to make sure all the numbers add up at the end of the year. Every business and most individuals need someone with the domain expertise to help prepare tax returns, especially time or resource-strapped small business owners. Majo Jacinto in his Udemy course provides an in-depth foundational understanding of how to prepare tax returns (and stay current with ever-changing laws) that'll certify you with tax prep skills in as little as a few hours of training and practice. Then once tax season rolls around you'll be able to charge an average of $229 per return as a freelance tax preparer with this side business idea, according to CNBC.

25

Remote English Teacher/Tutor

Teaching and tutoring English as a second language is a great way to make a solid side business idea work, not to mention opening doors for you to travel the world if you'd like. While full ESL (English as a Second Language) accreditation is recommended, as long as you're a native speaker, there are people in countries such as Hong Kong or the UAE who are willing to pay upwards of $25/hr for you to teach them English via Skype. Indeed, Learn4Good and Remote. co often have remote English tutoring jobs posted, check back frequently. Then once you land that remote job, you'll need somewhere more professional than your dining room table to meet with students—check out this post about how to find places to work remotely and you'll officially graduate this side business idea into a full-time endeavor for yourself.

26

SAT Tutor

If you had a knack for standardized tests and had no trouble acing the SAT, ACT, or other college exams, why not start tutoring high schoolers as a side business idea? Parents of all economic backgrounds are more than willing to shell out upwards of $100/hr to the right tutor if it means their son or daughter will get admitted to the college or university of their choice. See this quick checklist for starting an SAT tutoring business from the Work At Home Mom. Whitney over at Rookiemoms also has a cool story to share about a stay-at-home mom making $40/hr helping kids out with homework and turning it into a profitable side business idea.

27

Social Media Manager

We're all guilty of spending too much time on Facebook, Twitter, or Pinterest sometimes, so why not get paid to put your expertise to work as a side business idea? Lots of companies, especially startups or those in retail and travel—even influencers have heavy social media presences and are constantly in need of people to help build their brands online. You can find these types of opportunities on sites like Flexjobs and CareerBuilder and most employers on these websites are conditioned to work with people who operate these services as their side business idea. Over time as you grow in your ability to leverage various social channels, you can add more service offerings like running high-return Facebook Ad campaigns or hosting lucrative sweepstakes competitions for the brands you want to work with.

Build your own social following and create a personal brand for yourself like Matt Nelson, founder of WeRateDogs has done (thus growing his following to more than 2.8 Million people), and countless opportunities will come your way for turning this side business idea into a full-time business.

28

Google Paid Ad Specialist

If you know a thing or two about paid internet marketing and are comfortable with Google, a great way to make some extra income as a side business idea is to sign a freelance contract to manage a company's Google Ad Campaigns, and gradually start bringing on more clients as your consulting business grows. Just be sure to brush up on all the right business slang and industry jargon that's pervasive in the online marketing world before you launch unprepared into this side business idea.

29

Presentation Design Consultant

Yes, even the PowerPoint presentation requires outside consulting every now and then—especially if it's not your forte. I know I would happily outsource the visual layout of my presentation decks for work meetings, investor pitches, and lectures. Tobias Schelle of 24Slides is living proof that you can turn your skills at slideshow presentation design into a legit side business idea—and potentially earn up to $20 a slide for your time and talents.

30

Travel Consultant

If you love to travel and find yourself randomly searching for airfare sales or browsing Lonely Planet, why not carve out a niche for yourself as a private travel agent? Take my friend, Mark Jackson lead with what he's doing to build a travel consulting side business idea. Start with word-of-mouth recommendations from friends who know they can count on you for the cheapest flights, create a Facebook or LinkedIn group to invite people who want to stay on top of the latest deals, and eventually you could spin this business idea into a full-time consultancy teaching people how to make your dream trip a reality.

31

Landing Page Specialist

If you have a way with words and know how to make keyword-friendly, beautifully designed, SEO-optimized landing pages, why not charge other companies for your services and turn it into a money-making side business idea? Even a short landing page is worth a couple of hundred bucks in most cases, and so much more if you know how to pitch your prospects well. If you want to get started with your business idea of becoming a landing page specialist or freelance copywriter, check out Len Smith and Sean Kaye's awesome course on Udemy, Copywriting Secrets: How to Write Copy That Sells.

32

Interior Design Consultant

Someone out there is remodeling their kitchen and needs to know which shade of granite will match best with mahogany flooring. That someone will often be happy to pay you for your advice, especially if you're the kind of person that subscribes to websites like Contemporist and you have the motivation to turn this business idea into a money-making enterprise.

33

Housesitter

It's not exactly a way to make consistent great money, but housesitting—exactly what it sounds like—is a fantastically easy business idea that can fund your ability to live in exciting locales around the world (or your city) without paying a dime in rent. Did I mention it's a way to travel and live rent-free? Here's a list of four great websites from the legendary Nomadic Matt, to start your housesitting side business idea search.

34 Babysitter

No, babysitting isn't just for teenagers and college students. Quite on the contrary, if you call yourself an Au Pair instead, you can make some pretty good side money working nights and weekends with this business idea if you don't mind the often odd hours.

35

Property Manager

Know someone who rents out property to others? Perhaps they could use a hand managing their property. If so, you can make a decent amount of money on this side business idea with relatively little work on your part (most of the time). It'll take some hustling and the willingness to be flexible with your schedule, as you'll be responsible for collecting rent checks, managing repairs, and improvements, and simply being on call for emergencies. But, a property manager is essential for most real estate investors that have a large enough portfolio, so there's definitely merit to this business idea.

36

Sell on Etsy

Have a talent for crafting or creating other handmade goods? From bracelets to phone cases, rings, furniture, and more, Etsy is one of the world's largest independent marketplaces that's perfect for anyone who is creative and willing to sell their handmade creations. As long as you have the space, this can make for one of the best home business ideas that can be started as a side hustle with a very limited investment. Consider these 5 steps to starting an Etsy store, from Handmadeology. Then, after you're able to build your brand and grow your own audience, you can start an eCommerce site of your own and retain a larger portion of the revenue from your product sales—making this a very lucrative potential business idea if you're able to find an audience that loves your products.

37

Ebay Sales

Similar to selling on Amazon, eBay is a place to make money selling just about anything you can think of as a side business idea, with the added excitement of using the auction selling model to sometimes get way more than you expected for that antique baseball card you picked up at a local street fair. To turn your eBay selling into a legitimate business idea, look for opportunities where you can buy in-demand products at a discount—and later sell them for a profit. Eventually, you can even take the lessons learned from your eBay store and build a full-on blog or eCommerce business like what the team over at Gear Hungry has done.

38

Fiverr Gigs

***Fiverr** is a great place for first-time freelancers who might not have tons of experience and want to build up a portfolio of their work. You'll be able to complete simple tasks ranging from logo design to creating animations, or even drawing a company logo on your forehead. While this side business idea likely won't be growing into a million-dollar startup for you, it can still be a platform for funding your next big business idea. Want to learn more about Fiverr's history and how to get the most out of selling on the platform? Listen to my interview with Fiverr CEO Micha Kaufman.*

39

College Admissions Essay Editor

If editing and advising college students on how to write compelling 500-word essays on topics such as "You were just invited to speak at the White House. Write your speech," seems like a compelling business idea to allocate your free time towards, trust me—tons of parents will pay you to edit admissions essays and offer constructive feedback for their children. Be careful not to blur the ethical line of actually writing their essays, but serving as an editor to help them convey their message can become a great side business idea that has the potential to spread by word-of-mouth referral in your community.

40

Portrait Photographer

If you own a camera, starting a freelance portrait photography business could be a very natural way to turn your skills and passions into a profitable business idea. Start with doing free shoots for friends and family to build up a strong online portfolio, get familiar with your gear and the editing process, then you'll be able to get paid for photographing professional head shots and celebratory family moments as your side business idea. Get started by checking out this men's portrait photography class that regularly broadcasts for free on CreativeLive. Plus, once you have all the photography gear, you can earn a little extra side income by renting it out when you're not using it through online marketplaces like Fat Lama.

41

Wedding Photographer

Wedding photographers command premium rates. After all, you are capturing one of a couple's most important life moments, making it a very lucrative side business idea. Many professional wedding photographers charge between $2,500 - $10,000 (or more) to shoot a wedding, so it's realistic that this side business idea could quickly blossom into becoming a full-time endeavor with the right happy clientele base that's willing to refer you to their friends and family. Check out the Complete Wedding Photography Experience over on CreativeLive to get up to speed on everything you need to launch a successful wedding photography business.

42

Online Dating Consultant

Believe it or not, some people have such a difficult time with dating, that they don't even want to participate in the online (or app-based) component of it. If you're a smooth talker, why not leverage that skill into becoming a paid match maker as a side business idea?

43

Writing Erotic Fiction

Werewolves, step-brothers, and tentacles—the demand is high. As odd as it may sound, if you've got the imagination (and a clever pseudonym), you can make upwards of $5,000 a month writing erotic fiction in your free time as a side business idea.

44

Writing Greeting Cards

Fancy yourself a poet? You can earn $300 for every poem you write that this greeting card company publishes—not a bad side business idea if you've got a way with words and aren't afraid of rejection on poems that aren't a good fit.

45

WordPress Website Consultant

Countless small businesses start out their web presence using a WordPress-hosted website (myself included) before needing to upgrade to other solutions for various reasons. Many of them will pay several hundreds of dollars for someone to get their business idea set up online. If you have the patience to learn how to do it yourself, it's an extremely valuable skill and can be turned into a very lucrative side business idea—especially if you sign up for affiliate programs with companies like Kinsta, which offer high-quality managed WordPress hosting plans that allow you to collect fees from the clients you refer their way. Plus, with the skills you pick up from this side business idea, you'll be able to spin up other profitable website ideas like my friend Andy's been able to do with his site, AwesomeStuffToBuy.

46

Drive for Uber or Lyft

Driving for one of the two globally expanding app-centric taxi alternative services, Uber or Lyft can still be a fairly lucrative way to earn money as a side business idea on nights and weekends—working only when you want. But before you dive head first into this side business idea, do your homework and calculate the costs of extra gas, mileage, tires, wear & tear, and usage on your vehicle—it's not a guaranteed business idea that'll turn a huge profit every weekend.

47

Rent Your Car on Turo

If you own a car but barely use it, you can make some easy cash as an effortless side business idea by renting it out on Turo. Before you freak out, know that there's a $1 Million insurance policy on all cars, plus drivers are prescreened, so you can have peace of mind. Closely related to renting out your car is another new service I recently came across (available only in the UK at the moment) called YourParkingSpace where you can sign up to list your available parking space through the app, and earn when people decide to use your spot.

48

Art Collector

Not to be confused with hoarding, this business idea takes a lot of time, patience, and passion. If you have an eye for good art, it's easy to get in on the ground level by visiting the studio department at your local university—though don't expect to get rich overnight with this side business idea. Many art students are more than happy to sell their work for a bargain, and in as little as a few years, there's a chance that piece you bought for a couple hundred bucks may be worth well into the thousands. Beware though, this business idea will take a whole lot of patience (and storage space for all that art).

49

Catering Business

EatWith is a great way to test the waters as a chef for your side business idea, and if you have enough rave reviews you might be able to turn your knife skills into a full-time endeavor where you're leveraging your network to book catering events. This side business idea is built heavily upon getting happy referrals, so be sure to over-deliver for your first customers, and ask if they know anyone else who could be in need of your catering services.

50

Online News Correspondent

You don't need to have a degree in journalism to be a reporter these days (and pursue this business idea as a work-from-home job). Plus, there are many news websites that can always use a bit of help on getting local coverage. Some of them, such as The Examiner or HuffPost, will compensate contributors based on ad revenue generated per article written—a great incentive to provide compelling content to news organizations as your side business idea.

51

Patent Something

This side business idea isn't for most, but consider Kia Silverbrock who has been granted over 4,665 US Patents in his lifetime (so far). You don't have to invent the wheel to make good money from your patented concepts—just make sure that your idea can be produced affordably, or it will never stand up to a lawsuit in the future.

52

Buy and Sell Domain Names

Domain name trading has been around for the last couple of decades, and while most slam-dunk names have long been sold off (Insure.com went for $16 Million in 2009) there are still plenty of others that you can get your hands on for relatively cheap and broker as your side business idea. But beware: some experts doubt the long-term viability of this business idea, so you shouldn't quit your day job just to put all your effort into this one without some successes already in the bag. To get you started, here are some tips from GoDaddy, arguably the world's largest and most famous repository of domain names. Imagine owning desirable domain names for the next decade's most innovative companies.

53

Start a Popup Shop

While the barriers to entry for a retail shop can be very high, one way to keep costs down and limit your time investment while you keep your full-time job is to set up a weekend popup shop as a side business idea. More of whatever it is you're selling—donuts, clothing, antique baseball cards, or anything else—will stay in your pockets instead of going to pay for operating expenses such as rent or utilities by choosing to pursue retail as a side business idea with a short-term rental. This guide from Shopify will give you a step-by-step process for getting your popup shop off the ground.

54

Brew Your Own Beer

Like drinking beer? Why not try making it yourself as your side business idea? With enough patience and skill, you might end up brewing something that others are willing to pay to drink. Pick up an easy-to-use starter kit from Mr. Beer online, invest the time it'll take to perfect your craft, make a unique brew and start shopping it around to friends & family to see what they think of this side business idea.

55

Freelance Proofreading and Editing

As long as there is still the written word, there will always be editors. Freelance editing and proofreading not only pays a decent hourly wage but also gives you the chance to read about potentially interesting topics too. What's more, pursuing freelance writing & editing as a business idea can afford you a lifestyle that lets you travel the world as a digital nomad. You can find lots of job postings from companies and individuals in need of writing, proofreading, and editing services on Contena, which makes this a high-demand side business idea.

56

Buy Used Electronics and Refurbish Them

Many people give up on their faulty laptops, mobile phones, or cameras without even looking into the cause of their malfunctions. If you have the skills to fix them, consider pursuing this side business idea of refurbishing and reselling used electronics in your free time.

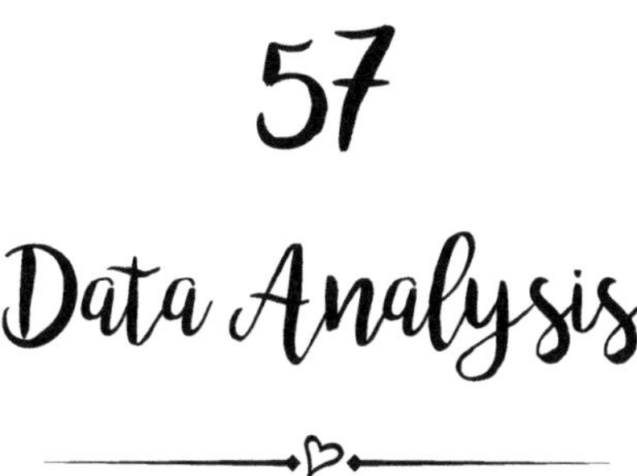

57 Data Analysis

Got a thing for numbers? Plenty of companies need to hire talented contractors who are good at data analysis, making this a potentially lucrative side business idea if you have the right credentials and experience. Platforms like Upwork and Digiserved are but two of many websites that are great for freelancers with analytical prowess, looking for extra work as a side business idea around their full-time jobs.

58

Acquire Parts from Electronics Stores

Believe it or not, there's a treasure trove of valuable items being thrown away by big box stores around the world. Electronics stores toss out everything from printer cartridges to tablets, and if you've got the stomach for rummaging around in dumpsters you can easily earn a bit (more than you ever thought possible) with this side business idea.

59

Freelance Writing & Copywriting

Every website owner (including myself) hires copywriters to write content for things like about pages, FAQs, or blog posts. Hourly wages for novice copywriters are not very high, but with some experience and a growing portfolio, you can become a freelance writer today and soon be charging more than you make at your full-time job if you find the right clients and brand yourself as an expert with this side business idea. Check out one of my most talented friends, Jory Mackay, for an example of someone who's doing a great job of positioning himself as a premium service provider with his freelance writing side business idea. Then when you're ready to start cold emailing potential clients, pick up my free downloadable freelance proposal template and get started today.

60

Licensed Product Distributor

It doesn't happen overnight, but licensing a foreign product for sale domestically, can be a lucrative business idea that (at times) leads to a big payoff down the road. Invest intelligently, sell a product you believe in, and you can reap the rewards for years to come.

61

Fill Out Online Surveys

It's not very engaging, or mentally stimulating, but taking online surveys through companies like Survey Junkie do pay out (a little), believe it or not. Even if the payouts come in the form of Amazon gift cards, sites like Swagbucks can pay well. Just don't expect to make bank with this side business idea—I recommend combining it with another source of side income from this list of my best business ideas, and turning to surveys in your downtime when you need a little extra income.

Not only is Airbnb a great way to make money by renting out your spare bedroom or living room couch as a legitimate home-based business idea, but you also have the benefit of meeting new people and making new friends if that's your kind of thing. You can even rent out an entirely new apartment just to manage as an Airbnb side business idea, but don't make the mistake of thinking this will be a passive source of income-you're on call whenever you have a guest and you'll always need to keep the place clean for incoming visitors. On top of just renting on Airbnb, you can take this business idea to the next level by offering your guests add-ons and personalized experiences for an extra charge. Take Lauren Gheysens' Airbnb-based side business idea, Royal Day Out in London, England for example—where she gives visiting tourists a local-only tour of the city, complete with bespoke 18th-century costumes.

63

Personal Fitness Trainer

If you're a fitness buff and have the right combination of charisma and business sense, working as a part-time personal trainer as a side business idea can be both physically and financially rewarding. Once you build up a reputation and client base for yourself, it could easily turn into a full-time endeavor for you. Check out these tips for a successful personal training business by the American Fitness Professionals and this interview with several fitness blog owners who are making a living online, from MonetizePros. Finally, I'd recommend checking out this resource if you want to take this business idea seriously and get started with a business plan for your personal fitness trainer business today.

64

Yoga or Meditation Instructor

Yoga is getting ever more popular, which means yoga instructors are more in demand than ever—making this another physically rewarding side business idea. Link up with a local yoga studio to teach nightly classes or offer personalized yoga in-home at a higher rate to pursue this kind of emotional and physical balance with others, during your free time while helping your bank balance, too.

If your mastery of another language is good enough to have the grammar and spelling down, translating is a great side business idea to set up for yourself and can even be done remotely. Flexjobs has literally hundreds of freelance, remote translator jobs available right now, and if you're looking to land more remote work on the side of your other pursuits.

66

Tour Guide

Live in a destination where travelers frequently visit? If you love meeting new people from around the world and also love the city you live in, starting your own local tour company is arguably the best business idea that will give you both of those perks. Take a unique spin on your local tour business like Erik from Vantigo. He was starting his VW van tour business in San Francisco as just a side business idea while he was still working a full-time job, and grew it to being a sustainable source of full-time income before quitting—now he's running a multiple van tour company on the back of what originally began as a crazy side business idea.

Scan to Connect with Me

Instagram

Twitter

LinkedIn

Printed by Libri Plureos GmbH in Hamburg,
Germany